SOCCER
AND ITS GREATEST PLAYERS

inside *sports*

SOCCER
AND ITS GREATEST PLAYERS

EDITED BY SHERMAN HOLLAR

Britannica®
Educational Publishing
IN ASSOCIATION WITH

ROSEN
EDUCATIONAL SERVICES

Published in 2012 by Britannica Educational Publishing
(a trademark of Encyclopædia Britannica, Inc.)
in association with Rosen Educational Services, LLC
29 East 21st Street, New York, NY 10010.

First Edition

Britannica Educational Publishing
Michael I. Levy: Executive Editor, Encyclopædia Britannica
J.E. Luebering: Director, Core Reference Group, Encyclopædia Britannica
Adam Augustyn: Assistant Manager, Encyclopædia Britannica

Anthony L. Green: Editor, Compton's by Britannica
Michael Anderson: Senior Editor, Compton's by Britannica
Sherman Hollar: Associate Editor, Compton's by Britannica

Marilyn L. Barton: Senior Coordinator, Production Control
Steven Bosco: Director, Editorial Technologies
Lisa S. Braucher: Senior Producer and Data Editor
Yvette Charboneau: Senior Copy Editor
Kathy Nakamura: Manager, Media Acquisition

Rosen Educational Services
Hope Lourie Killcoyne: Senior Editor and Project Manager
Nelson Sá: Art Director
Cindy Reiman: Photography Manager
Karen Huang: Photo Researcher
Matthew Cauli: Designer, Cover Design
Introduction by Hope Lourie Killcoyne

Library of Congress Cataloging-in-Publication Data

Soccer and its greatest players / edited by Sherman Hollar.
    p. cm. —(Inside sports)
"In association with Britannica Educational Publishing, Rosen Educational Services."
Includes bibliographical references and index.
ISBN 978-1-61530-516-2 (library binding)
1. Soccer—Juvenile literature. 2. Soccer players—Juvenile literature. I. Hollar, Sherman.
GV943.25.S62 2011
796.334—dc22

                                                                    2011000893

Manufactured in the United States of America

On the cover, page 3: Lionel Messi. *Denis Doyle/Getty Images*

Pages 6-7, 85, 88, 92, 93 © www.istockphoto.com/Adam Kazmierski; pp. 10, 20, 29, 54, 84 © www.istock-
photo.com/Sebastian Vera; pp. 16, 17, 18, 22, 26, 27 © www.istockphoto.com/Justin Skinnerback; back
cover and remaining interior background image Shutterstock.com

CONTENTS

INTRODUCTION

What's in a name? When it comes to the world's most popular team sport, the designation you use generally signifies where you come from. Americans refer to it as soccer, those in Spanish-speaking countries say *fútbol*, and much of the rest of the English-speaking world calls it football. Technically, the official title is association football. Clearly, football, fútbol, and association football are all of a linguistic piece—so where does the word *soccer* come from? It actually originated more than one hundred years ago in England as a slang abbreviation based on the *soc* in association. In Australia, the wordplay game has been taken one step further, as the national team there is nicknamed the Socceroos, a melding of *soccer* and *kangaroo*.

Because soccer is the world's most popular sport, it follows then that the game's premier international tournament, the World Cup, played every four years, would be the world's most popular sporting event, and indeed it is. Soccer also has the distinction of being the first team sport to have been included in the Olympics as an official event, an honor it gained in 1900.

Readers of this book will learn of soccer's earliest roots in China, Greece, and North America and of the modern game's emergence in 19th-century England. But it was a group of European countries other than Great Britain that first attempted to bring international order to the game, when, at the turn of the 20th century, the Fédération Internationale de Football Association (FIFA) was formed. Of course, rules evolve, and FIFA—as a governing body responsive to hundreds of national associations worldwide—occasionally releases modifications or clarifications of those rules. FIFA does so in concert with the International Football Association Board (IFAB).

Scoring the opening goal in a game is always something to celebrate, and here Shinji Kagawa of Borussia Dortmund (left) does just that with his teammates during a match against Sevilla, on Dec. 15, 2010, in Seville, Spain. David Ramos/Getty Images

But as any fan of the game knows, clear rules and diligent officiating by referees notwithstanding, the football pitch (aka soccer field) has been host to a good deal of theatrics over the years. Players have been known to try to incur a penalty against the opposing team by using various forms of body language to convince officials of the grievous wrong done them: lying flat on the ground or writhing in pain are two popular options for this desired outcome. Vigorously objecting to either a yellow or red card are also prime opportunities for on-field drama. But theatrical embellishments aside, as with any physical, aggressive, and demanding sport, true injuries are always a very real possibility, and in a game such as this—where body-protecting equipment is at a minimum—players must take care to be on their guard.

Players must also be in top shape, for soccer is a physically demanding sport. A taxing game consisting of two 45-minute halves played straight through with a 15-minute break in between, it has spawned dazzlingly athletic stars the world over, many of whom are profiled in this book. From Franz Beckenbauer to Zinédine Zidane and David Beckham to Cristiano Ronaldo, soccer's all-time legends and current stars are showcased within.

Whatever you happen to call it—fútbol, football, association football, or soccer—to paraphrase legendary player Pelé, it is a beautiful game, by any name.

CHAPTER 1

THE GAME OF SOCCER

The game of soccer, or association football, as it is properly called, is the world's most popular team sport. Virtually every country on Earth plays the game. It has been estimated that at the turn of the 21st century there were some 240 million soccer players around the globe and more than 1.3 billion fans. One of the reasons that soccer is so appealing is because of its simplicity. A ball and a bit of open space are all that is required to play, and there is really only one essential rule—players cannot touch the ball with their hands. Many people are drawn to the athletic skill and quick thinking that soccer requires. Brazil's Pelé, perhaps

Soccer teams line up in a generally standard formation, though variations are used to increase offense and defense. **Encyclopædia Britannica, Inc.**

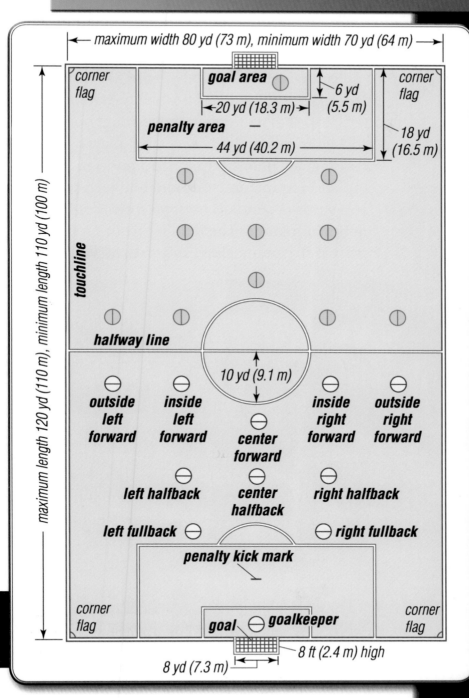

maximum width 80 yd (73 m), minimum width 70 yd (64 m)

corner flag

goal area

6 yd (5.5 m)

20 yd (18.3 m)

corner flag

penalty area

18 yd (16.5 m)

44 yd (40.2 m)

maximum length 120 yd (110 m), minimum length 110 yd (100 m)

touchline

halfway line

10 yd (9.1 m)

outside left forward

inside left forward

center forward

inside right forward

outside right forward

left halfback

center halfback

right halfback

left fullback

right fullback

penalty kick mark

corner flag

goal

goalkeeper

corner flag

8 ft (2.4 m) high

8 yd (7.3 m)

the greatest player the sport has ever known, called soccer "the beautiful game."

Rules established by the Fédération Internationale de Football Association (FIFA), the worldwide governing body of soccer, require that soccer be played on a rectangular field between 100 and 130 yards (90 and 120 meters) long and between 50 and 100 yards (45 and 90 meters) wide. For international matches the field is 110 to 120 yards (100 to 110 meters) long and 70 to 80 yards (64

World-renown goalkeeper Petr Čech of the Czech Republic slides into action during the FIFA 2010 World Cup qualifier match against Northern Ireland, on Oct. 14, 2009. Having sustained a near-fatal head injury in 2006, Čech wears not only the standard goalie garb but protective headgear as well. **Alexander Hassenstein/Getty Images**

to 73 meters) wide. A goal 8 yards (7.3 meters) wide and 8 feet (2.4 meters) high is placed at each end of the field. The lines marking the sides of the field are the touchlines; those on either end are the goal lines. The field has distinctive markings for the halfway line, the goal areas, the penalty areas, the corners, and the center circle.

The uniforms usually consist of shorts, a shirt with a number, socks, shoes with cleats, and shin guards. Goalkeepers typically wear padded shorts and gloves and must wear a shirt that is noticeably different from the other players'.

The ball is a round, inflated rubber bladder covered with leather or some other approved material. It measures between 27 and 28 inches (68 and 70 centimeters) in circumference and weighs between 14 and 16 ounces (410 and 450 grams).

HOW THE GAME IS PLAYED

The purpose of the game is to propel the ball into the opponents' goal using only the feet, head, or body. Only the goalkeepers can touch the ball with their hands. The team scoring the most goals wins. There are 11 players to a team—a goalkeeper and ten field players divided into defenders (fullbacks), midfielders (halfbacks), and forwards. Players advance the ball by passing (kicking or heading the ball to a teammate) or dribbling the ball downfield. (In dribbling, the player controls the ball with the feet.) The ball may also be kept moving by juggling—using one's thighs, chest, or shoulders as well as the feet or head.

Toni Calvo of Aris Thessaloniki FC (football club) stands back as Bayer Leverkusen's Arturo Vidal juggles the ball during a match on Nov. 4, 2010. **Christof Koepsel/Bongarts/Getty Images**

Defensive players will try to stop the opposition by intercepting passes or by tackling. In soccer, a "tackle" occurs when a player steals the ball from the feet of another player.

Players run as many as 6 or 7 miles (10 or 11 kilometers) during the course of a game. The game is officiated by a referee, who enforces the rules and keeps track of the time, and two linesmen, who patrol the touchlines and determine possession. A game lasts 90 minutes and is divided into halves; the half-time interval lasts 15 minutes, during which the teams change ends. Additional time may be added by the referee to compensate for stoppages in play (for example, player injuries). If neither side wins, and if a victor must be established, "extra-time" is played, and then, if required, a series of penalty kicks may be taken.

The offside rule and fouling are two of the most common and important calls made by game officials. The offside rule requires that an offensive player not pass the two defenders closest to the goal until the ball is played to him (the last defender being the goalie). The rule prevents players from lurking about the goal all game, but it can be difficult to judge. When offside is called, a free kick is awarded to the defensive team.

OFFSIDES

Simply being in an offside position—that is, being an attacker beyond the next-to-last defender of the opposing team—does not itself amount to a violation. A penalty is called only if the attacking (offensive) player does any of the following:

- Tries to play a ball passed to him or her
- Attempts to prevent the opposing team from playing the ball (for instance, obstructing the sight line of the goalie by standing in the way)
- Indirectly benefits from being offsides (such as receiving a rebound of a ball hitting against a goalpost or crossbar).

Soccer is a physical game, but fouls are called when the play becomes too rough. Typically a foul results in a free kick for the opposition. When a foul is particularly rough, the referee may give a yellow card warning to the offending player. A player receiving two yellow cards in a game is automatically given a red card and ejected from the game. Violent behavior, such as fighting, can lead to an immediate red card.

POSITION SKILLS

Soccer's most basic skill is the use of the feet and legs to control and pass the ball. Heading the ball is also important, particularly when receiving long aerial passes. Although players often display their individual skills by going on "solo runs" or dribbling the ball past opponents, soccer is essentially a team game based on passing between team members. Players are credited with an assist when they make a pass to a teammate that results in a score.

The basic styles and skills of individual players reflect their respective positions. Goalkeepers need to have agility and height to reach and block the ball when opponents shoot at goal. Central defenders, who are called upon to win tackles and to head the ball away from danger such as when defending corner kicks, are usually big and strong. Fullbacks are typically smaller but quicker— traits necessary to match speedy forwards. Midfield players may have a range of qualities: powerful "ball-winners" need to be "good in the tackle" in terms of winning or protecting the ball, while creative "playmakers" develop scoring chances through their talent at holding the ball and through accurate passing. Wingers, who set up scoring opportunities for forwards, must have good speed and dribbling skills and the ability to make crossing passes. Forwards can be powerful in the air or small and penetrative with quick footwork; essentially, they should be adept at scoring goals from any angle.

Defender Massimo Paci of Italy's Parma FC moves the ball with his head in a December 2010 match. **Claudio Villa/Getty Images**

Malaysia's team captain Safiq Rahim, playing for his country against China during the second round of the Guongzhou 2010 Asian Games, reacts to being red carded by referee Ben Williams. Liu Jin/ AFP/Getty Images

When an offensive player is fouled in the penalty area, his or her team is awarded a penalty kick, which is taken from a spot 12 yards (11 meters) in front of the goal. Only the goalkeeper is allowed to defend against a penalty kick and, not surprisingly, these kicks most often end up in the goal.

CHAPTER 2

HISTORY AND ORGANIZATION OF SOCCER

Soccer has a history that stretches back centuries, although the modern game can be said to have originated in England in the 1800s. By the early 20th century, soccer was being played in many parts of Europe, and with the establishment of FIFA, the game was poised to expand worldwide.

ORIGINS AND DEVELOPMENT OF THE GAME

Various civilizations lay claim to inventing the sport of soccer. There are records of soccerlike games having been played in China more than 2,000 years ago as well as in ancient Greece and North America. "Folk football," a game played throughout Europe in which competing teams would attempt to move a ball toward a final destination, provided the origin of most football games, including soccer. The folk football games were played over vast areas and often pitted one village against another. The games were also quite violent, and local governments often tried to ban the sport.

England, however, was the real starting place of the modern game of soccer. Variant types of football were played in English schools, where soccer and rugby alike find their roots. The Football Association (FA) was created in 1863 to establish and maintain uniform rules of play. In 1872 the first international game was played between England and Scotland, and it was in England that soccer professionalism was legalized in 1885. At the turn of the 19th century, agents of the British Empire helped to spread the sport to every corner of the globe. The Football League was formed in England by 1888 and became a model for league play elsewhere. A typical European soccer league featured a top division, in which the very best teams played, and two or three lower divisions. Teams finishing at the top of their division were promoted to the next level, while teams at the bottom were demoted. Nationwide club tournaments, such as the FA Cup in England, also became prevalent.

PASSION, RIVALRIES, AND HOOLIGANISM

The advent of television and the Internet has helped to fuel soccer's rise in popularity. Soccer fans are among the most passionate in all of sport. Club teams often have strong regional or ethnic identities, and intense rivalries are common. In Glasgow, Scotland, for instance, the Roman Catholic–identified Celtic club and the Protestant-identified Rangers enjoy one of the sport's oldest and greatest rivalries. Unfortunately, the passion of soccer fans has sometimes crossed the line into violent, antisocial behavior. In the 1960s and '70s such behavior exploded into a major problem for the sport. Certain fans, known as hooligans, organized into groups with a primary goal of stirring racial intolerance and violence against fans of rival clubs. Improvements in security and facilities, as well as active campaigns by clubs and other soccer fans to promote tolerance and sportsmanship, have helped to combat the hooligan problem.

During a 2004 friendly match between Germany and Switzerland—the term "friendly" connoting a game without consequence relative to ranking—this German hooligan was decidedly unfriendly as he shouted racist slogans throughout the game. The word "troublemaker" can be seen tattooed on his belly. **John MacDougall/AFP/Getty Images**

A goalie (wearing the same color uniform as his teammates) catches the ball above his head in this painting of a football match by English artist William Heysham Overend, created circa 1900. **Popperfoto/ Getty Images**

ORGANIZATION AND COMPETITION

Although soccer had spread across Europe by the early 20th century, it was still in need of international organization. A solution was found in 1904, when representatives from the football associations of Belgium, Denmark, France, the Netherlands, Spain, Sweden, and Switzerland founded FIFA. Today the governing body, which is headquartered in Zürich, Switzerland, has more than 200 member nations and oversees the activity of millions of players worldwide.

Soccer has been played in every Summer Olympics since 1900, except the 1932 Games in Los Angeles. The true world championship, however, is the FIFA-run World Cup.

The 2010 World Cup was played in South Africa. Here, Landon Donovan of the United States celebrates his goal against Algeria with teammate Edson Buddle. FIFA's post-tournament ranking had the United States in 12th place. Timothy A. Clary/AFP/Getty Images

It is played every four years and is the most-watched sporting event in the world.

FIFA instituted World Cup tournaments for men under the age of 21 in 1977 and an under-17 Cup in 1985. A World Cup for women debuted in 1991, and a women's under-19 World Cup was introduced in 2002 (later changed to an under-20 tournament). A women's under-17 World Cup was inaugurated in 2008.

FIFA membership is open to all national associations. They must accept FIFA's authority, observe the laws of association football, and possess a suitable infrastructure (that is, playing facilities and internal organization). FIFA statutes require members to form continental confederations. The first of these, the Confederación Sudamericana de Fútbol (commonly known as CONMEBOL), was founded in South America in 1916. In 1954 the Union of European Football Associations (UEFA) and the Asian Football Confederation (AFC) were established. Africa's governing body, the Confédération Africaine de Football (CAF), was founded in 1957. The Confederation of North, Central American and Caribbean Association Football (CONCACAF) followed four years later.

WORLD CUP

The first World Cup was organized by FIFA in 1930. The event was won by Uruguay, which also hosted the competition. National teams from 13 countries participated in the inaugural World Cup. Today, the competition consists of preliminary qualifying tournaments leading to a final elimination event made up of 32 national teams. Six FIFA continental confederations oversee the preliminary tournaments in their respective regions. Unlike the Olympic men's soccer competition—which is limited to players

Guessing which way to dive to block a penalty kick is something of an inexact art. Here, in the final match of the 2006 World Cup, French goalkeeper Fabien Barthez dives the wrong way, allowing Italy's Fabio Grosso to score the match-winning goal. **Mike Hewitt/Getty Images**

aged 23 and under, with each team allowed three players over 23—World Cup teams are not limited to players of a certain age. All players participating in World Cup competition must be citizens of the country they represent. Referees for the World Cup are selected from lists that are submitted by all of the FIFA-affiliated national associations, which in the early 21st century numbered more than 200.

With the exception of 1942 and 1946, when World War II prevented the tournament from being held, the World Cup has been played every four years since 1930. From 1930 to 1970 the trophy cup that was awarded to the World Cup champions was the Jules Rimet Trophy, named for the Frenchman who proposed the tournament. This cup was permanently awarded in 1970 to then three-time winner Brazil (1958, 1962, and 1970), and a new trophy called the FIFA World Cup was put up for competition.

The World Cup has experienced remarkable growth in popularity since the tournament's inception and in the 21st century continues to attract global attention. The 2002 World Cup, which was held in South Korea and Japan in what marked the first dual hosting of a World Cup final tournament, drew a cumulative television audience estimated at more than 26 billion people. The 2006 World Cup in Germany attracted a similarly sized television viewership, with some 715 million people around the world tuning in to watch the dramatic final match in which Italy beat France 5–3 in a penalty shoot-out. South Africa hosted the 2010 World Cup, the first time that the event was held in an African country. Brazil is scheduled to host the 2014 World Cup.

The Oceania Football Confederation (OFC) appeared in 1966. These confederations may organize their own club, international, and youth tournaments, elect representatives to FIFA's Executive Committee, and promote soccer in their specific continents as they see fit. In turn, all players, agents, leagues, national associations, and confederations must recognize the authority of FIFA's Arbitration Tribunal for Football, which effectively functions as soccer's supreme court in serious disputes.

CHAPTER 3
SOCCER LEGENDS

Although soccer is essentially a team game, players often have opportunities to showcase their individual talents. Throughout the history of the modern game, there have been certain players who stand out above the rest—and a special few who have elevated their sport to unprecedented heights. Beckenbauer, Cruyff, Pelé, Maradona—these players and others who are discussed on the following pages are among the hallowed figures of soccer and are truly deserving of being called legends of the game.

FRANZ BECKENBAUER

German soccer player Franz Beckenbauer is the only man in the history of association football to have both captained and managed World Cup–winning teams. He also won the

European Footballer of the Year award twice (1972, 1976). Known for his authoritative and elegant style, Beckenbauer was nicknamed der Kaiser ("the Emperor"), and he dominated the field with precise touches and great changes of pace.

Beckenbauer was born on Sept. 11, 1945, in Munich. He joined Bayern Munich in 1959 and made his first-team debut in 1963. As captain from 1971, he helped Bayern win three European Champions Clubs' Cups (1973–74, 1974–75, and 1975–76) and four national titles. Beckenbauer debuted in a World Cup in England in 1966. Though der Kaiser scored four goals, Germany lost the final match against the host country.

Four years later, Beckenbauer had another chance against England during the quarter-finals of the 1970 World Cup, scoring one goal in Germany's victory over the defending champions. Germany moved on to the semi-final game against Italy—a match known as the "Game of the Century." With Italy winning by one goal, Beckenbauer charged over an Italian defender, falling on the field and dislocating his right shoulder. The German side tied the game in the last minute, forcing the match into overtime. Beckenbauer continued playing with his arm in a sling strapped to

West German team captain Franz Beckenbauer celebrates as his team defeats the Netherlands 2-1 during the 1974 World Cup final. **Popperfoto/Getty Images**

his body. Italy eventually defeated Germany 4–3, with five goals in extra time, but the bravery of Beckenbauer became legendary.

During the 1974 World Cup in Germany, Beckenbauer led Germany to the final against the Netherlands. Germany won the game 2–1, and Beckenbauer became the first captain to lift the brand-new FIFA World Cup trophy. (Brazil had retained the Jules Rimet Trophy in 1970.) Beckenbauer retired from playing in 1983 and a year later was named Germany's head coach. He returned to the World Cup in 1986, taking his team to the final game against Argentina. An inspired Diego Maradona was too much for the German team, however, and Beckenbauer had to wait four more years for another chance. At the 1990 World Cup in Italy, Germany won the title undefeated.

GEORGE BEST

In the 1960s and early '70s, George Best electrified English soccer fans with his thrilling goal-scoring runs while playing for Manchester United. Born on May 22, 1946, in Belfast, Northern Ireland, Best was spotted at age 15 by a scout who reported to Manchester United coach Matthew Busby that he had found a "genius." Best promptly signed with United and in 1963 made his debut in England's first division. In his career with United, he scored 178 goals in 466 appearances. Perhaps his best year was 1968, when he was named Footballer of the Year in both England and Europe and scored the key goal in a 4–1 victory over Benfica of Portugal in the European Cup final. The handsome, shaggy-haired Best was often called the "fifth Beatle"

George Best of Manchester United sails past a defender in this 1968 game. **Bob Thomas/Getty Images**

as he became a leading figure in the swinging culture of 1960s England. His star began to fade, however, as his drinking began to take a toll on his overall fitness and the quality of his play. After a bitter departure from United in 1974, he played for numerous lesser teams in the United Kingdom, Spain, Australia, and the United States. His drinking continued to affect his play, however, and he became as well known for his squandered talent as for his undeniable brilliance. Best underwent a liver transplant in 2002 but was unable to overcome his alcoholism. He died on Nov. 25, 2005, in London.

JOHAN CRUYFF

Dutch soccer player Johan Cruyff epitomized the concept of "total football"—a style of play that emphasized all-around skill, versatility, and creativity. He was that rare player who possessed the ability to do everything on the field: pass, shoot with both feet, head the ball, defend, attack, and set the timing of the game.

Cruyff was born on April 25, 1947, in Amsterdam. His mother did the cleaning for Amsterdam's Ajax soccer club and convinced the coaches to give him a chance on the club's youth development squad. Cruyff joined the youth team at age 10 and made his debut with the club's senior team at 17. In his next season, he scored 25 goals in 23 games, giving Ajax the first of eight Dutch league championships under his leadership. In the following years, Ajax had one of the most astonishing runs in soccer history, winning three consecutive UEFA Champions

Leagues, one Intercontinental Cup, and two UEFA Super Cups. Cruyff crowned these years by winning the European Footballer of the Year award on three occasions (1971, 1973, and 1974).

Cruyff transferred to Barcelona in 1973. With Cruyff as captain, Barcelona won the Spanish League championship in 1974 and was runner-up in 1976 and 1977. At the 1974

Johan Cruyff escorts the ball during the 1974 World Cup in Germany.
Bob Thomas/Getty Images

World Cup tournament the Dutch team, led by Cruyff and including Johan Neeskens and Ruud Krol, put on a memorable display of total football. Although the Netherlands lost to West Germany in the championship match, Cruyff's individual brilliance won him the tournament's Most Valuable Player award.

Cruyff retired from playing in 1984 and took the job of Ajax head coach in 1986. Under his command, Ajax won two Dutch Cups and one UEFA Cup. This run earned him a post as coach in Barcelona, where he became the most successful coach in the history of the Spanish team, winning 11 titles, including four leagues, the UEFA Cup, and the UEFA Champions League.

JULIE FOUDY

A star player with the U.S. women's national soccer team, Julie Foudy ruled the American midfield with tireless energy and determination, playing 271 games during her 17-year career with the team. As cocaptain of the U.S. squad from 1991 to 2000 and as the team's sole captain from 2000 to 2004, Foudy was a leading figure in the "Golden Era" of women's soccer, alongside her teammates Mia Hamm, Joy Fawcett, and Kristine Lilly.

A triumphant Julie Foudy holds the trophy after winning the Women's Gold Cup final against Brazil in 2000. **Al Bello/Getty Image**

Foudy was born in 1971 in San Diego, California. Her prodigious talents on the soccer field were evident early. By the age of 16 she had become a member of the U.S. women's team, and she was voted High School Player of the 1980s by the *Los Angeles Times*. She scored her first World Cup goal in 1991 during a quarterfinal match against Chinese Taipei, and six days later, she gave the United States its first Women's World Cup title. In 1995 the United States finished in third place at the World Cup in Sweden but returned to the winners' circle at the 1996 Olympic Games in Atlanta. At the 1999 World Cup, Foudy was a key player in the legendary American run for the cup that ended in a thrilling penalty shoot-out against China. At the 2000 Olympics in Sydney, Australia, the Americans took home the silver medal, but led by Foudy, they again won gold at the 2004 Olympics in Athens, Greece.

Foudy retired from playing in 2004. She later founded the Julie Foudy Sports Leadership Academy, where she helped young players to become role models on and off the field. In 1997 she became the first American soccer player to receive the FIFA Fair Play Award for her work against child labor. In 2007 Foudy was inducted into the U.S. National Soccer Hall of Fame.

MIA HAMM

By any measure, the playing career of American soccer superstar Mia Hamm was astonishing. FIFA twice named her the Women's World Player of the Year (2001–02). A powerful striker, she scored more international goals (158) than any other player—male or female— in the history of the sport. Aside from her knack for goal-scoring, Hamm was revered for her all-around skill and competitive spirit.

Hamm was born in 1972 in Selma, Alabama. At the age of 15 she became the youngest player ever to join the U.S. women's national team, and at 19 she was the youngest member of the U.S. squad that won the World Cup in China in 1991. She was a star of the U.S. team that captured the gold medal at the 1996 Olympics in Atlanta. In 1999 she scored her 109th international goal, breaking the all-time record. During the 1999 World Cup, Hamm led the U.S. team against China in the legendary final game of that tournament. The game had finished scoreless, and the two nations faced off in a penalty shoot-out. Hamm made one of the penalty shots that set up her teammate Brandi Chastain to score the game-winning penalty kick, and the U.S. national team lifted its second World Cup trophy.

Mia Hamm dribbles upfield in the FIFA Women's World Cup final against China on July 10, 1999. Jed Jacobsohn/Getty Images

Hamm announced her retirement at the end of the 2004 Olympics in Athens. She scored twice during the tournament and took the team to the final against Brazil. The United States won the game 2–1, and Mia Hamm left soccer with a new gold medal on her chest. In December 2004, after having played 275 games with the U.S. national team, Hamm hung up her boots for good. In Hamm's first year of eligibility, she was voted into the U.S. National Soccer Hall of Fame in 2007.

DIEGO MARADONA

The top player of the 1980s and one of the greatest of all time, Argentine soccer star Diego Maradona was renowned for his ability to control the ball and create scoring opportunities for himself and others.

Maradona was born on Oct. 30, 1960, in Lanús, Argentina. A soccer prodigy, he became the star of the youth team of Argentinos Juniors at age 12, and he debuted on the professional team ten days before turning 16. In 1981 he joined Boca Juniors and quickly led the team to the league championship. He then moved to Europe, playing with Barcelona in 1982 (and winning the Spanish Cup in 1983), then Napoli (1984–91).

Diego Maradona of Argentina and a South Korean defender face off in a 1986 World Cup game. **Colorsport**

With Maradona the Naples side won the league title and cup in 1987 and the league title again in 1990.

Maradona's career with the Argentine national team included World Cup appearances in 1982, 1986, 1990, and 1994. At the 1982 World Cup in Spain, he scored two goals and helped his team move to the second round, but Italy and Brazil defeated Argentina and sent the team home empty-handed. The World Cup in 1986 was a different story. As captain of the Argentine team, he was the most dominant player of the tournament. In Argentina's quarterfinal match against England, he scored what has been described as the "Goal of the Century," taking the ball in his own half and sprinting by five English players before dribbling past the goalie and kicking the ball into the net. Maradona led his team to victory in the World Cup final against Germany, providing the assist for the winning goal.

Maradona repeated his role as captain of the Argentine team in the 1990 World Cup. Argentina lost the final match after the Germans scored a penalty kick five minutes before the end of the game. In the 1994 World Cup, Maradona played only two games before being sent home after failing a drug test for ephedrine doping. In 2007 Maradona declared that he had recovered from his drug addiction and pledged to focus again on soccer. In 2008 he became head coach of the Argentine national team and in

2010 led it to the quarterfinals of the World Cup in South Africa.

PELÉ

"Soccer in its purest form" was played by Pelé, a South American superstar who was the world's most famous and highest-paid athlete when he joined a North American team in 1975. He led the Brazilian national soccer team to three World Cup victories in 1958, 1962, and 1970 and to permanent possession of the Jules Rimet Trophy.

Edson Arantes do Nascimento was born to a poor family on Oct. 23, 1940, in Três Corações, Brazil. He began playing for a local minor-league club when he was a teenager. He made his debut with the Santos Football Club in 1956. With Pelé at inside left forward, the team won several South American clubs' cups and the 1962 world club championship.

Pelé scored his 1,000th goal in 1969. The legendary athlete retired in 1974 but made a comeback in 1975 after accepting a reported 7-million-dollar contract for three years with the New York Cosmos of the North American Soccer League. He said he came out of retirement not for the money, but to "make soccer truly popular in the United

Pelé, one of the game's most dynamic and imaginative athletes, played for the short-lived New York Cosmos in the mid 1970s. **Focus on Sport/Getty Images**

States." His farewell appearance was against his old Santos club in 1977.

Pelé, whose nickname does not mean anything, became a Brazilian national hero and was also known as Pérola Negra (Black Pearl). An average-sized man, he was blessed with speed, great balance, tremendous vision, the ability to control the ball superbly, and the ability to shoot powerfully and accurately with either foot and with his head.

In his career he played in 1,363 matches and scored 1,281 goals. His best season was 1958, when he scored 139 times. In addition to his accomplishments in sports, he published several best-selling autobiographies, starred in several documentary and semidocumentary films, and composed numerous musical pieces, including the entire sound track for the film *Pelé* (1977). He was the 1978 recipient of the International Peace Award, and in 1999 he was named athlete of the century by the International Olympic Committee.

MICHEL PLATINI

Players who wear jersey number 10 are usually leaders with the ability to orchestrate their team. And there is no doubt that French superstar Michel Platini was the perfect number 10.

Born in 1955 in Jœuf, France, Platini began his playing career in 1972 with AS Nancy. He helped Nancy win the French Cup in 1978. He left the club for Saint-Étienne in 1979, after he and the French national team failed to pass the first round at the World Cup in 1978 in Argentina. His days with Saint-Étienne were a mixed success. The team won the French League in 1981 but failed to advance in two European cups.

French footballer Michel Platini playing for Italy's Juventus during a 1985 match. **Allsport/Getty Images**

Things changed for Platini in the 1980s. After joining the Italian team Juventus, he helped the team win the Italian Cup, the Italian League twice, and the UEFA Champions League. Individually, Platini won the top scorer award in Italy three years in a row and was named European Footballer of the Year three consecutive times: 1983, 1984, and 1985.

On his way to the 1982 World Cup, Platini formed the so-called *carré magique* ("magic square") of the French national team with teammates Alain Giresse, Luis Fernández, and Jean Tigana. It was one of the most talented midfields ever assembled. France advanced to the Cup semifinals against Germany. Germany scored first, but Platini answered quickly, scoring a penalty. The game went into overtime and, after 120 minutes, had to be decided in a penalty shoot-out. Once again, Platini scored, but two other French players missed. France couldn't reach the final. But redemption came two years later, when Platini led the French to victory in the 1984 European Championship. Platini was in splendid form, scoring nine goals in five games.

Platini returned to the World Cup in 1986, scoring two goals, but France lost again in the semifinal against Germany. In June 1987

Platini hung up his boots for good. In January 2007 he was named UEFA president.

RONALDO

Brazilian soccer player Ronaldo possesses a phenomenal athleticism that combines strength, speed, and well-honed skill. In 1996 Ronaldo became the youngest soccer player ever to receive the FIFA World Player of the Year award.

Ronaldo Luis Nazário de Lima was born on Sept. 22, 1976, in a suburb of Rio de Janeiro. When he was 15 years old Ronaldo made his professional debut as a forward with the team Cruzeiro in the city of Belo Horizonte, north of Rio. Ronaldo scored 58 goals in 60 games for the club. He then moved to Europe to play for the Dutch club PSV Eindhoven. Ronaldo was sold to Spanish club Barcelona in 1996. During his single season with Barcelona he made 34 goals in 37 games and led the team to victory at the European Cup–Winners' Cup before transferring to the Italian club Internazionale of Milan. Ronaldo finished the 1997–98 season as the second-leading scorer in Italy's Serie A league, with 25 goals in 32 matches.

Ronaldo made his Brazilian national team debut in March 1994. At the 1994 World Cup

...es during a Corinthians training session on May 19,
...ena/LatinContent/Getty Images

he watched from the sidelines as his country's team won the championship. Two years later, Ronaldo played an active role in Brazil's bronze-medal win at the 1996 Olympic Games. He led Brazil to victory at the 1997

Copa América against Bolivia. He also helped his team win the 2002 World Cup in Japan.

In 1997 FIFA again named Ronaldo World Player of the Year. He was also recognized as World Player of the Year in 2002. At the 2006 World Cup he scored three goals to bring his career total at the tournament to a record-setting 15. While playing for AC Milan in 2008, Ronaldo ruptured a tendon in his left knee, which some thought would put his career in jeopardy. In December 2008 a fully recovered Ronaldo signed with the Corinthians in São Paulo. However, he continued to be plagued by a number of other, less significant, leg injuries during his time with the Corinthians, as well as by a thyroid condition that made him gain weight, and he abruptly retired from the sport in February 2011.

ZINÉDINE ZIDANE

French soccer player Zinédine Zidane was one of the game's most talented attacking midfielders. He is one of only two men—the other being Ronaldo—to have been named FIFA World Player of the Year three times.

Zidane was born of Algerian parents in Marseille, France, in 1972. He began his career with AS Cannes at age 17. In 1992 he joined

Bordeaux, and four years later he became part of legendary club Juventus in Italy. The French national team called Zidane in 1994, and he quickly became the key playmaker on the team. In 1998, with France hosting the World Cup, Zidane and the talented French side captured the World Cup title by defeating Brazil 3–0 in the final. Two years later, Zidane scored two goals to lead France to the 2000 European Championship (Euro). He was chosen as the FIFA World Player of the Year in 1998 and 2000.

Despite this outstanding record, one trophy remained elusive for the French superstar—the UEFA Champions League. Zidane had two chances to win the cup with Juventus, but the team lost two finals in a row in 1997 and 1998. Zidane joined Real Madrid in 2001, and the following year the team won the UEFA Champions League title as well as the European Super Cup. FIFA again selected Zidane as World Player of the Year in 2003.

Injury kept Zidane from shining at the 2002 World Cup, and after France failed to reach the finals of the 2004 Euro, Zidane retired from the national team. He rejoined the team for the 2006 World Cup, however, and took France to the final against Italy. He scored a quick goal, but the match went into

Zinédine Zidane dribbles the ball during the final match of the 2006 World Cup. **Bloomberg via Getty Images**

overtime, during which Zidane head-butted an Italian defender. Zidane was sent off, and France lost the game in a penalty shoot-out. Despite his red card, Zidane was awarded the Golden Ball as the best player of the tournament. He retired from professional soccer after that game.

CHAPTER 4

CURRENT STARS

A number of soccer players have emerged in recent years who have won championships and performed extraordinary feats on the field and who many observers already rank among the finest players in the game's history. These are today's superstars, and they continue to excite soccer fans around the world with their thrilling and innovative play.

DAVID BECKHAM

A gifted midfielder, English soccer player David Beckham is perhaps best known for his free kicks and crosses. His shots often appear to "bend" around players from the other team.

David Robert Joseph Beckham was born on May 2, 1975, in London. During the 1995–96 season he helped Manchester United win the Premier League title and the Football

Association (FA) Cup. The following year Manchester United successfully defended its league title, and Beckham was voted Young Player of the Year. In the 1998–99 season Manchester won the league title, the FA Cup, and the European Cup, and Beckham was named the UEFA Best Midfielder and the UEFA Club Footballer of the Year. He went on to help Manchester win three more Premier League championships (2000, 2001,

David Beckham, captain of the English team, celebrates after scoring in the 2006 World Cup. Though England lost in the quarterfinal stage, the goal made Beckham the only British player to score in three consecutive World Cups. **Bob Thomas/Getty Images**

2003). The 2002 film *Bend It Like Beckham* paid homage to his kicking ability.

In 1999 Beckham married singer Victoria Adams, best known as "Posh Spice" of the Spice Girls pop group. The intense media attention to the couple increased Beckham's popularity around the world. Beckham led England's national team to appearances in the World Cup in 1998, 2002, and 2006. In 2006 he made history by becoming the only player from England's national team to score a goal in three consecutive World Cup tournaments.

After the completion of the 2002–03 season, Beckham left Manchester United. He joined the Spanish soccer club Real Madrid. Four years later he moved to the United States to play for the Los Angeles Galaxy. In October 2008 Beckham signed a deal to play with the Italian team AC Milan during the Galaxy's off-season. A tear to Beckham's left Achilles tendon knocked him out of competing in the 2010 World Cup. Beckham was inducted into the English Football Hall of Fame in 2008.

DIDIER DROGBA

Didier Drogba of Côte d'Ivoire came late onto the soccer scene, signing a professional contract at age 21 and having his first successful season at 23. But once he found his form, the power- ful striker became a lethal goal scorer who changed the history of his small West African country.

Drogba was born on March 11, 1978, in Abidjan, Côte d'Ivoire. He moved to France at the age of five, and at 18 he joined Le Mans in the French Ligue 2. Team Guingamp offered him a

Didier Drogba, a prolific goal scorer, is one of the star players of Chelsea FC, "The Blues." **Mike Hewitt/Getty Images**

chance in the Ligue 1, and the Ivorian quickly responded with 20 goals in two seasons. A year later, Drogba joined Marseille, where he became a fan favorite, but it wasn't until July 2004 that Drogba attracted widespread attention with his transfer to England's Chelsea FC. He led the team to their first-ever Premier League title in 2005, guiding them to a successful defense of the title a year later. In addition, he was the key player in Chelsea winning both the Football Association (FA) Cup and the Carling Cup trophies during the 2006–07 season. In 2009 Chelsea won its second FA Cup with Drogba on the squad. The following year Chelsea won both the FA Cup and the Premier League title, with Drogba leading the league in goals—29 for the season.

In the international arena, Drogba captained Côte d'Ivoire to its first-ever World Cup appearance, in 2006, a feat that turned him into a national hero. A few months after the World Cup, Drogba was named African Footballer of the Year. Drogba led Côte d'Ivoire to a fourth-place finish in the 2008 Cup of Nations, and he was again selected as African Footballer of the Year in 2009. Côte d'Ivoire qualified for its second consecutive World Cup in 2010.

SAMUEL ETO'O

Samuel Eto'o was the first player to be named African Footballer of the Year three consecutive times (2003–05). He is the all-time leading scorer in the history of the African Cup of Nations.

Born on March 10, 1981, in Nkon, Cameroon, Eto'o was called to the national team at age 14. When he played in the 1998 World Cup, he was, at the age of 17 years and 3 months, the youngest player in the tournament. Four years later, he scored his first World Cup goal. With an outstanding positional awareness, speed, and shooting technique, Eto'o was a key member of the Cameroonian squad during the team's championship runs at the African Cup of Nations in 2000 and 2002. His impressive play continued at the 2000 Olympic Games in Sydney, where Cameroon defeated Spain for the first Olympic gold in the nation's history. Eto'o was the leading scorer in the 2008 African Cup of Nations with five goals. It was during that tournament that he became the top scorer in the competition's history with a tally of 16.

After having played with Real Madrid of the Spanish League, Eto'o signed with Real

Samuel Eto'o of FC Internazionale Milano prepares to strike on Oct. 29, 2010. The Cameroon forward was named African Player of the Year for 2010, his fourth time winning that title. **Massimo Cebrelli/ Getty Images**

Mallorca in 2000 and became that club's all-time leading goalscorer. He was lured to FC Barcelona in 2004. Barcelona won Spanish first-division championships in 2005 and 2006, as well as the Champions League in 2006. Eto'o led Barcelona to a historic season in 2009, when the club captured its first "treble" by winning the national first-division title, Spain's major domestic cup (Copa del Rey), and the Champions League. At the end of the season, Eto'o was transferred to FC Internazionale (Inter Milan).

THIERRY HENRY

Fast, powerful, and a master in one-on-one situations, Thierry Henry is one of the most exciting players to watch on a soccer field and is considered one of the most prolific goalscorers of his era.

Born of Antillean parents in the suburbs of Paris in 1977, Henry made his debut with Monaco in 1994 and went on to help the team win the 1997 French club championship. An uneventful season with Italian powerhouse Juventus followed in 1998, but it was after his transfer to Arsenal in England that Henry became an international superstar. He earned the Golden

Boot award as Europe's leading scorer for two consecutive years. With Henry on the attack, Arsenal won two Premier Leagues and three FA Cups. With 226 goals, he became Arsenal's all-time leading scorer. Arsenal fans were heartbroken when the team announced that Henry was leaving to join FC Barcelona in 2007.

Playing with the French national team, Henry scored three goals in the first two games of the 1998 World Cup en route to helping France lift the first World Cup trophy in its history. The team quickly went on to win a second international trophy at the 2000 European Championship, with Henry ending the tournament as the team's top scorer. All this raised the expectations for the 2002 World Cup, but France and Henry failed to score a single goal in the tournament and exited the cup in the first round.

France returned to the 2006 World Cup and made it into the final against Italy, but France lost the game in penalty shoot-outs. In October 2007 Henry became France's top scorer of all time, passing team legend Michel Platini. In 2010 Henry was released by Barcelona and subsequently signed with the New York Red Bulls of Major League Soccer.

Thierry Henry of the New York Red Bulls gets the ball p
Matt Pickens of the Colorado Rapids during a match on
Andy Marlin/Getty Images

KAKÁ

Known for his forceful all-around skills, Brazilian forward Kaká possesses superior ball control, great speed, and impressive technique. His extraordinary range of talents enabled him to become FIFA's World Player of the Year in 2007.

Ricardo Izecson dos Santos Leite was born on April 22, 1982, in Brasília. Kaká is a common term of endearment for the name "Ricardo" in Brazil, and this is what his younger brother started calling the future soccer star. Kaká made his first-team debut with São Paulo in January 2001. In 2002 he debuted on the Brazilian national team, and later that year Brazil won the World Cup. Three years later, he was a major player on the Brazilian squad that conquered the 2005 Confederations Cup, scoring the second goal of the game in the final against Argentina.

In 2003 Kaká signed with AC Milan in Italy. The Brazilian made an immediate impact, scoring 10 goals in 30 games and leading the team to the Italian Serie A title and the European Super Cup in his first season. He had another great year with Milan in 2006, scoring three hat tricks during the season, including one during the UEFA Champions League. These performances set the scene for the 2006 World Cup in Germany. Expectations were high after Kaká scored the winning goal in Brazil's opening match. Although the Brazilians reached the quarterfinals, they were eliminated by France.

In 2007 Kaká powered Milan to the UEFA Champions League final against Liverpool.

Real Madrid midfielder Kaká plays at a home game against Mallorca in January 2010. **Dominque Faget/AFP/Getty Images**

He provided the assistance for Milan's second goal of the match and helped the team capture Europe's most prestigious tournament. Although he professed a desire to finish his career in Milan, Kaká transferred to Real Madrid in June 2009.

MARTA

Many think that Brazilian soccer star Marta is the most exciting player in the history of the women's game. Marta Vieira da Silva, who was born in 1986 in the small city of Dois Riachos in eastern Brazil, joined her first club, Vasco da Gama, in Rio de Janeiro at age 14. By the time Vasco da Gama disbanded its women's team in 2001, Marta had begun to make a name for herself, finishing as the top scorer in a Brazilian youth tournament. She later played with the club Santa Cruz before joining the Swedish team Umeå IK in 2004. In her four seasons with Umeå IK, Marta found the net an astonishing 111 times.

Marta is a gifted left-footed midfielder who moves to the attacking position with great timing and vision. Although Marta was FIFA's World Player of the Year in 2006, it was during the 2007 Pan American Games that many fans in Brazil discovered her stunning game. Marta was the tournament's top scorer, netting 12 goals, and led Brazil to the gold medal. She was brilliant in the final game held at the famous Maracanã stadium in Rio, where she attracted comparisons to the legendary Pelé.

Marta scores a penalty shot for Brazil in the team's quarterfinal match against Australia during the 2007 Women's World Cup. Paul Gilham/Getty Images

Led by Marta, the Brazilian women's team reached the World Cup final in 2007. Although Brazil lost the final game against Germany, Marta had one of the most impressive individual performances in the history of the World Cup, scoring seven goals and taking home the Golden Ball Award as the best player in the tournament. That year she picked up her second consecutive FIFA World Player of the Year award. She also earned the award in 2008 and 2009. After four years in Sweden, Marta moved to the United States to play in the newly formed Women's Professional Soccer league.

LIONEL MESSI

Soccer prodigy Lionel Messi of Argentina has impressed fans and rivals alike on any field where he has had a chance to show his skills. Fast, smart, and bold, Messi can do anything with the ball. And he started doing it at very young age. Born in 1987 in Rosario, Argentina, he was attracting attention with his soccer talents by the age of five. At age 13 Messi and his family relocated to Barcelona, and three years later he was given his informal debut with FC Barcelona in a friendly match. In the 2004–05 season, Messi, then 17, became the youngest official player and goal scorer in the Spanish La Liga (the country's highest division of association football).

The fast-moving Messi, only 5 feet 7 inches (1.7 metres) tall and 148 pounds (67

Argentinian-born forward Lionel ("Leo") Messi dribbles between two Nigerian defenders during the Olympic soccer final at the Beijing Games in 2008. **AFP/Getty Images**

kg), is called La Pulga (the Flea) by his team-mates. Selected to play with the Argentine national team during the 2006 World Cup, Messi became the youngest player ever to represent Argentina at that event. Messi returned to international action during the 2007 Copa América. He turned in an impressive performance and was named the best young player of the tournament. At the 2008 Olympics in Beijing, Messi scored two goals during Argentina's run to the gold medal.

During the 2008–09 season, Messi helped Barcelona capture the club's first treble — the La Liga championship, the Copa del Rey, and the Champions League title. He scored 38 goals in 51 matches during that season and was named FIFA World Player of the Year. During the 2009–10 season, Messi scored 34 goals in domestic games as Barcelona repeated as La Liga champions, and he earned the Golden Boot award as Europe's leading scorer.

BIRGIT PRINZ

Widely regarded as the finest European women's soccer player of the 1990s and 2000s, Birgit Prinz was named the FIFA Women's World Player of the Year for three

Birgit Prinz of Germany during the women's international friendly match between Germany and China, Feb. 28, 2008. **Vladimir Rys/ Bongarts/Getty Images**

consecutive years (2003–05), the first player to achieve that feat.

Prinz was born in 1977 in Frankfurt am Main and at age 16 made her international debut for Germany as a 72nd-minute substitute in a game against Canada; she scored in the 89th minute to secure a 2–1 victory for Germany. A natural striker with great speed and ball control, Prinz quickly became a star in the women's Bundesliga, the top soccer division in Germany. Prinz's teams claimed four European championships, two UEFA Cups, eight German league championships, and eight domestic cup trophies. In 2002 she played a season in the United States for the professional Women's United Soccer Association (WUSA) team Carolina Courage, helping them win the WUSA championship before she returned to Germany.

In addition to her three World Player of the Year awards and several Olympic bronze medals (2000, 2004, and 2008), Prinz played on two World Cup-winning German national teams (2003 and 2007). In the 2007 World Cup final against Brazil, Prinz opened the scoring in the 52nd minute on the way toward a 2–0 win for Germany. It was a record 14th goal in World Cup matches for Prinz.

Prinz also received much praise for her activities off the field. She has actively participating in FIFA's campaign against racism, and she has visited children in war-affected areas in Afghanistan as a patron of the Learn and Play Project supported by FIFA, the National Olympic Committee, and Afghanistan Aid.

RONALDINHO

Ronaldinho is Portuguese for "Little Ronaldo," and this soccer wizard really began to shine at a very young age. He was born in Porto Alegre, Brazil, in 1980, and by age 13 he had begun to attract media attention with his spectacular performances, including scoring 23 goals in a single game. Soon thereafter he became a world champion, leading the Brazilian team to victory in the 1997 under-17 World Cup in Egypt.

The soccer world was captivated by Ronaldinho's skills, speed, and all-around exceptional talent. After winning the under-17 Cup, he next conquered the 1999 Copa América and arrived at the 2002 World Cup as a rising superstar. Ronaldinho didn't disappoint, emerging as one of the best players

Brazilian forward Ronaldinho leads AC Milan in 2010. Giuseppe
Cacace/AFP/Getty Images

in the tournament and helping Brazil win its fifth World Cup title.

In 2003 Ronaldinho joined FC Barcelona. In his first two seasons with Barcelona, he won the La Liga trophy twice, and by 2004 he was named FIFA World Player of the Year, a feat he repeated in 2005. That same year, Ronaldinho lifted his first Confederation Cup with Brazil, and in 2006 he won the UEFA Champions League with Barcelona.

By the end of 2006, Ronaldinho had won every major soccer tournament on the planet. Unfortunately, the talented Brazilian failed to make an impression during the 2006 World Cup, and he was not included in the Brazilian team that won the 2007 Copa América. He signed a three-year contract with AC Milan in 2008 and quickly became a starting player on the Italian team. His Brazilian teammate Kaká departed Milan in June 2009, leaving Ronaldinho to lead the team.

CRISTIANO RONALDO

In January 2009 Cristiano Ronaldo became the first player from Manchester United to receive FIFA's World Player of the Year

Cristiano Ronaldo holds his 2008 FIFA World Footballer of the Year award. **Fabrice Coffrini/AFP/Getty Images**

award. Born in Madeira, Portugal, in 1985, Ronaldo started playing soccer when he was 9 years old. He debuted on Sporting Clube de Portugal's first team in 2002 and signed with Manchester United the following year, becoming the first Portuguese to join the celebrated British squad.

Ronaldo was an instant sensation with United and soon came to be regarded as one of the best forwards in the game. His finest season with the team came in 2007–08, when he scored 42 League and Cup goals and earned the Golden Boot award as Europe's leading scorer, with 31 League goals. He led United to a Champions League title in May 2008 and fueled the team's run to the 2009 Champions League final, which they lost to FC Barcelona.

In addition to his success with United, Ronaldo was a staple of the Portuguese national team since his debut in August 2003. Portugal was the host of the 2004 European Championship, during which Ronaldo scored two goals and helped his side reach the final against Greece. But Ronaldo and Portugal failed to score against the Greeks and lost 1–0. Two years later, Portugal proved to be one of the most spectacular teams in the 2006 World Cup, with Ronaldo helping the squad to a fourth-place finish.

In the spring of 2009, the soccer world was shaken when Spanish team Real Madrid announced that Ronaldo was leaving Manchester United to join the Spanish powerhouse for a record-breaking transfer of $132 million. The transfer made Ronaldo the most expensive player in soccer history.

WAYNE ROONEY

Wayne Rooney rose to international soccer stardom as a teenager while playing with Manchester United. Born on Oct. 24, 1985, in Liverpool, England, Rooney made his professional debut with his local club Everton at age 16, becoming the youngest goal scorer in Premier League history in his first season (the record has since been surpassed). After two years playing for Everton, he transferred to Manchester United in 2004. With Manchester the precocious young striker quickly became one of the most popular soccer stars in the United Kingdom.

Rooney was named England's Young Player of the Year in each of his first two seasons in Manchester. In 2006–07 he helped lead United to a Premier League

A high-spirited Wayne Rooney of Manchester Unit *his winning goal in a November 2010 match against* *Rangers.* **Alex Livesey/Getty Images**

championship and a victory in the Carling Cup. He was a key contributor to United's Premier League and Champions League titles in the 2007–08 season, which were followed by the team's first FIFA Club World Cup championship. Rooney and Manchester United won a third consecutive league title the following season. In 2010 he was named both the Professional Footballers' Association Player of the Year and the Football Writers' Association Footballer of the Year as the best player in English association football for the 2009–10 season.

Rooney was named a member of the English national team in 2003 and that year became—for a time—both the youngest player and the youngest goal scorer in England's history. He starred on an England squad that advanced to the quarterfinals of the 2004 European Championship (Euro 2004), but a slow recovery from a foot injury limited his effectiveness in the 2006 World Cup finals, where he went scoreless. England failed to qualify for Euro 2008, but Rooney led his country in scoring in qualifying matches for the 2010 World Cup.

FERNANDO TORRES

Spanish striker Fernando Torres scored the goal that returned his country to soccer glory. It happened during the final match of

Fernando Torres, who traded his red Liverpool shirt for Chelsea blue, is seen here in his first game for Chelsea, played on February 5, 2011, a 1 - 0 win for Liverpool. **Glyn Kirk/AFP/Getty Images**

the 2008 European Championship (Euro) against Germany. Although Spain had been a powerful soccer nation since the beginning of the 20th century, the country had won only one important international title—the 1964 Euro. That changed when Torres used his tremendous speed to win a ball over a German defender and netted the winning goal that gave Spain a 1–0 victory and the coveted Euro title.

Torres was born in Madrid in 1984. He joined Atletico de Madrid at age 11, and he debuted in the second division in 2001. By the time he was 19 he was Atletico's captain. Torres went on to play in the 2006 World Cup, scoring three early goals and giving Spain a promising start. But the Spanish team couldn't keep the momentum and lost its second-round game against France. Although Spain was sent home, Torres had made such a good impression that many European teams scrambled to sign the powerful striker. Liverpool, one of the most successful clubs in England, had the best offer, and Torres signed with his new team in March 2008. In his first year with the Reds, Torres established a new team record as the most prolific foreign goalscorer in a debut season, scoring 24 times. After only a year and a half with the team, he was included on a list published by the *Times of London* as one of the 50 greatest Liverpool players. Torres returned to the Spanish national team for the 2010 World Cup and helped lead Spain to its first-ever World Cup title.

In January 2011 Torres left the Reds for the Blues, transferring from Liverpool to Chelsea FC. The Spanish striker, nicknamed El Niño, or "the Kid," moved mid-season to Chelsea for a stunning £50 million ($80 million) transfer.

The enormous popularity of soccer around the world shows no signs of diminishing anytime soon. At the 2010 FIFA World Cup in South Africa, some 85,000 spectators filled the Soccer City Stadium in Johannesburg to watch Spain beat the Netherlands 1–0 in the final match. As was the case during the previous World Cup in 2006, more than 700 million additional fans watched the match on television. What explains soccer's global popularity? There are countless reasons for the enduring appeal of the sport, including the inherent excitement and drama of soccer competitions, the phenomenal abilities of the game's top players, and the passionate rivalries between teams and clubs that have developed over the years. The essential simplicity of soccer also cannot be overlooked. The mere fact that the sport can be played almost anywhere, from official playing fields to gymnasiums, streets, playgrounds, parks, or beaches, is one of the key reasons that soccer has been embraced in virtually every part of the world, making it certain that "the beautiful game" will be played for generations to come.

advent A coming into being or use.

bladder A synthetic pouch that can be blown up with air.

circumference The surface or outer limits of a sphere or rounded body; the measure of the perimeter of a great circle or sphere.

cleat A projecting piece that furnishes a grip, as with the rubber cleats on the underside of a soccer shoe.

debut A first appearance.

ephedrine An herbal stimulant derived from the plant ephedra. Believed to help with weight problems and boost energy levels, it was eventually shown to have severe side effects and has been linked to the deaths of scores of users, including several professional athletes.

epitomize To serve as the typical or ideal example of.

hallowed Sacred, revered.

hooligan A person who engages in rowdy, violent, or destructive behavior; in soccer, hooligans have often been responsible for organized violence in the stands, usually consisting of assaults on fans of other teams.

induct To admit as a member.

lurk To be constantly present or persist in staying; remain, linger.

overtime Time beyond or in excess of a set limit.

playmaker A player who leads the offense for a team; midfield players typically serve this role in soccer.

precocious Exceptionally early in development or occurrence.

prodigious Exciting amazement or wonder.

prodigy A highly talented child or youth.

prolific Marked by abundant inventiveness or productivity.

rupture To create a tear or breach in an organ or structure.

side In Britain, a synonym for team, as in "a football side."

squander To lose through negligence or inaction; waste.

stoppage The act of stopping or the state of being stopped; halt or obstruction.

tendon Cord of tissue that attaches the end of a muscle to a bone or other part of the body.

touchline Either of the lines that mark the sides of the field of play in rugby and soccer.

treble Set or group consisting of three parts; in soccer, a team that wins three trophies during a season is often said to have achieved a treble.

unprecedented Novel or new.

variant Different from others of its kind or class; exhibiting slight difference, alteration, or disagreement.

versatility The capacity to adapt to or embrace a variety of subjects, fields, or skills.

Canadian Colleges Athletic Association
   (CCAA)
St. Lawrence College
2 Belmont Street, Windmill Point
Cornwall, ON K6H 4Z1
Canada
(613) 937-1508
Web site: http://www.ccaa.ca
The CCAA provides information on college
   athletics throughout Canada as well as
   rankings, scores, and regulations.

The Canadian Soccer Association
Place Soccer Canada
237 Metcalfe Street
Ottawa, ON K2P 1R2
Canada
(613) 237-7678
Web site: http://www.canadasoccer.com
The Canadian Soccer Association is the
   governing body of soccer in Canada and
   offers information on men's and women's
   teams throughout the country.

Fédération Internationale de Football
   Association (FIFA)
FIFA-Strasse 20
P.O. Box 8044
Zurich, Switzerland

Web site: http://www.fifa.com
FIFA is the governing body of football
(soccer) worldwide and determines the
rules and regulations followed interna-
tionally. News, player statistics, game
and World Cup information, and a host
of other soccer-related items are also
available.

Major League Soccer (MLS)
420 Fifth Avenue
7th Floor
New York, NY 10018
(212) 450-1200
Web site: http://www.mlssoccer.com
MLS is a professional soccer league in the
United States for men and provides
information on players, schedules,
scores, and more.

The National Collegiate Athletic
Association (NCAA)
700 W. Washington Street
P.O. Box 6222
Indianapolis, IN 46206
(317) 917-6222
Web site: http://www.ncaa.org
The NCAA site provides information on
college athletics in the United States and

addresses issues facing student-athletes. It also offers information on NCAA-sponsored scholarships for students and post-graduates.

U.S. Soccer Federation
1801 S. Prairie Avenue
Chicago, IL 60616
(312) 808-1300
Web site: http://www.ussoccer.com
The U.S. Soccer Federation is the governing body of soccer in the United States. The site provides information on the men's national team, the women's national team, youth national teams, and the federation's development academy.

Women's Professional Soccer (WPS)
1750 Montgomery Street
1st Floor
San Francisco, CA 94111
(415) 553-4460
Web site: http://www.womensprosoccer.com
WPS is the highest level North American professional soccer league for women and provides information on players, schedules, and its WPS camps for women of all ages.

WEB SITES

Due to the changing nature of Internet links, Rosen Educational Services has developed an online list of Web sites related to the subject of this book. This site is updated regularly. Please use this link to access the list:

http://www.rosenlinks.com/spor/socc

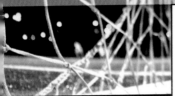

Adamson, Heather. *Let's Play Soccer* (Capstone Press, 2006).

Armstrong, Gary. *Football in Africa: Conflict, Conciliation, and Community* (Palgrave Macmillan, 2008).

Armstrong, Gary, and Giulianotti, Richard, eds. *Fear and Loathing in World Football* (Berg, 2001).

Galeano, Eduardo, and Fried, Mark. *Football in Sun and Shadow* (Fourth Estate, 2003).

Gifford, Clive. *Soccer* (PowerKids Press, 2009).

Giulianotti, Richard. *Football: A Sociology of the Global Game* (Blackwell, 1999).

Lopez, Sue. *Women on the Ball: A Guide to Women's Football* (Scarlet Press, 1997).

Murray, Bill. *The World's Game: A History of Soccer* (Univ. of Illinois Press, 1996).

Taylor, Chris. *The Beautiful Game: A Journey Through Latin American Football* (Indigo, 1999).

Walvin, James. *The People's Game: The History of Football Revisited*, 2nd ed. (Mainstream, 2000).

Maradona, Diego, 29, 32, 41–44
Marta, 66–68
Messi, Lionel, 68–70
midfielders (halfbacks), 14, 17

N

Neeskens, Johan, 36
New York Cosmos, 44–45
New York Red Bulls, 62

O

Oceania Football Confederation (OFC), 28
offside rule, 15, 16
Olympics, soccer in the, 24, 26, 38, 39, 41, 50, 59, 70, 72

P

Pelé, 10–12, 29, 44–46, 66
penalty areas, 13, 19
penalty kicks, 15, 19
Platini, Michel, 46–49, 62
position skills, 17–18
Premier League, 54, 55–56, 58, 62, 78–79
Prinz, Birgit, 70–73

R

Real Madrid, 52, 56, 59, 65, 78
Real Mallorca, 59–61
red card, 16, 53
referees, 15, 27
rivalries, and soccer, 22, 84
Ronaldinho, 73–75
Ronaldo, 49–51
Ronaldo, Cristiano, 75–78
Rooney, Wayne, 78–80

S

soccer
    current stars of, 54–83
    how game is played, 13–19
    legends of, 29–53
    official name of, 10
    organization and competition, 23–28
    origins and development of, 20–21
    popularity of, 10, 22, 27, 84
Spain, as World Cup winner, 83, 84

T

tackling, 15, 17
Tigana, Jean, 48